Autobiographies You Thought You'd Read

Count Dracula

Catherine Chambers

raintree

a Capstone company — publishers for children

Raintree is an imprint of Capstone Global Library Limited, a company incorporated in England and Wales having its registered office at 7 Pilgrim Street, London, EC4V 6LB – Registered company number: 6695582

www.raintreepublishers.co.uk
myorders@raintreepublishers.co.uk

Edited by Linda Staniford
Designed by Steve Mead
Original illustrations © Capstone Global Library 2015
Illustrated by Christian Suarez - Advocate Art
Production by Victoria Fitzgerald
Originated by Capstone Global Library
Printed and bound in China by Leo Paper Products

ISBN 978 1 406 29628 0 (hardback)
19 18 17 16 15
10 9 8 7 6 5 4 3 2 1

ISBN 978 1 406 29633 4 (paperback)
20 19 18 17 16
10 9 8 7 6 5 4 3 2 1

British Library Cataloguing in Publication Data
A full catalogue record for this book is available from the British Library.

Acknowledgements
Every effort has been made to contact copyright holders of material reproduced in this book. Any omissions will be rectified in subsequent printings if notice is given to the publisher.

All the internet addresses (URLs) given in this book were valid at the time of going to press. However, due to the dynamic nature of the internet, some addresses may have changed, or sites may have changed or ceased to exist since publication. While the author and publisher regret any inconvenience this may cause readers, no responsibility for any such changes can be accepted by either the author or the publisher.

Contents

Some words are shown in bold, **like this**. You can find out what they mean by looking in the glossary.

I am Count Dracula

"Aagh! Slurp, slurp. Yum! Ha! Ha! Ha!"
You're not frightened? Shame!
For I am Count Dracula,
a fearsome vampire.
I sink my fangs into
human flesh.
I suck tasty blood
from my victims.
Then they become
vampires, too.
I create chaos and
enjoy leading
people to grisly
deaths.

DID YOU KNOW?

Dracula means 'son of a dragon'.

Where do I come from?

Some people say I am invented by Bram Stoker, a writer in Victorian times. He said that I live in a mountainous region called Transylvania, in Romania.

DID YOU KNOW?

Bram Stoker (1847–1912) was an Irish writer. He wrote a popular novel called *Dracula* in 1897.

When was I born?

In Stoker's story, I am already hundreds of years old. He said I am related to Attila the Hun. Now, Attila really did have a taste for blood. He even killed his own brother, Bleda!

DID YOU KNOW?

Attila (about AD 410–453) ruled the **Hunnic Empire** in Europe from AD 440 to 453.

Where do I live?

According to Stoker, I live in a fine castle perched high on a cliff. It's a fairytale castle with turrets and **ramparts**. Down below, a fast flowing river runs through a deep **gorge**.

DID YOU KNOW?

When Bram Stoker imagined Dracula's castle, he was possibly describing Bran Castle in Transylvania. But Stoker had never visited it.

Why am I called Dracula?

Did Stoker name me after Vlad III Dracula, Prince of Wallachia? After Vlad died, people started calling him Vlad Țepeș, which meant Vlad the **Impaler**.

People say that Vlad pinned his enemies to the ground by putting a stake through their bodies. But according to Stoker, I too am terrified of the stake!

How bad was Vlad?

Was Vlad bloodthirsty? Oh yes. Vlad cut off the arms, legs and even noses of his enemies! He left people out in the cold where wild animals chewed them up. And some say he even drank blood...

DID YOU KNOW?

Vlad ruled Wallachia three times from the 1440s to the 1470s. He was always fighting his troublesome **nobles**.

What do I do?

I really like using my powers. I can **hypnotize** people. That's how I get them to let me into their homes. I can **shapeshift** into bats, wolves and creepy mist, too.

In Stoker's story, I try to get to London where millions of tasty people live. That's a lot of blood to drink! Delicious!

Do I live in a scary place?

Are there lots of scary, ghostly beings like me in Transylvania? Well, there are hairy werewolves. These wolf-like humans come out at night and eat dead bodies. Brilliant!

DID YOU KNOW?

Villagers near Bran Castle once believed in *strigoi*. These creepy witches left their bodies at night and haunted people.

What other bad things do I do?

Well, I cook up wicked spells. In Stoker's story, I **shapeshift** into a dog and stow away on a Russian ship. My magic makes it sink near a town in England called Whitby. Then I hop ashore and hunt down my victims.

Tourists visit Whitby to see the places mentioned in the *Dracula* story.

Where do I keep my victims?

In Stoker's story, I catch my victims and imprison them in my castle. I chain them up and suck their blood until they die. Then they become my vampire servants.

I have to keep killing people and sucking their blood. That way, I can live forever!

What can go wrong?

As you can see, I'm supposed to be pretty powerful. But in Stoker's story, humans begin to find my weaknesses. They discover that my powers are weak between sunrise and sunset.

Also, they work out that I can only sleep in the same soil that my family is buried in. I can't stay anywhere without it. And I'm terrified of garlic. Aagh!

Have I conquered the world?

Sadly, no. In Stoker's story, I get stabbed. Three vampires living in my castle are killed, too. Some people say that's the way to purify vampires' homes.

So everyone thinks I'm dead. We shall see about that! But what about Vlad? Did he die?

What happened to Vlad?

Vlad was killed by **Ottoman Turks**. But they did not act alone. A Transylvanian **warlord** and some **nobles** helped them. What a lot of enemies! But was Vlad really killed? Maybe he's now a ghostly vampire. Maybe, just maybe, he's me!

DID YOU KNOW?

Real blood-sucking creatures include vampire bats, **leeches**, torpedo snails, vampire squids, vampire **finches** and plenty of insects!

Glossary

finch type of bird

gorge deep narrow passage with steep rocky sides

Hunnic Empire empire formed by Attila the Hun, around the modern-day country of Hungary

hypnotize control someone's brain after putting them in a sleep-like state

impaler someone who sticks things to a surface by staking them with a sharp object

leech blood-sucking slug-like creature

noble powerful person of high rank in a kingdom

Ottoman Turk Turkish soldier from the Ottoman Empire in the Mediterranean

rampart flat-topped defensive wall

shapeshift change shape, e.g. from a human into an animal

warlord military leader of a warring country

Find out more

You could find out more about mythical vampires and real blood-sucking creatures in other books and on the internet.

Books

Top 10 Mythical Creatures, Lori Polydoros (Capstone Press, 2012)
Find out more about mythical creatures in this book.

Vampire Bats, Giant Insects, and Other Mysterious Animals of the Darkest Caves (Extreme Animals in Extreme Environments), Kindle Edition, Ana Maria Rodriguez (Enslow Publishers, 2013)
This book tells about animals that live in caves.

Websites

www.aquariumofpacific.org/onlinelearningcenter/species/vampire_squid
Find out about the vampire squid on this web site.

http://science.howstuffworks.com/science-vs-myth/strange-creatures/vampire5.htm
You will learn a lot about the origins of vampire legends on this web site.

kids.nationalgeographic.com/animals/vampire-bat.html
This web site will tell you about the habits of vampire bats.

Index